Practical
Meditation

Practical Meditation

Spiritual Yoga for the Mind

Sister Jayanti

Health Communications, Inc.
Deerfield Beach, Florida

www.hci-online.com

**Cataloging-in-Publication Data is on file with the
Library of Congress.**

©2000 Brahma Kumaris
ISBN 1-55874-827-X

Publisher: Health Communications, Inc.
            3201 S.W. 15th Street
            Deerfield Beach, FL 33442-8190

Cover design by Andrea Perrine Brower
Inside book design by Dawn Grove

CONTENTS

FOREWORD

Practical *Meditation* is highly recommended for those who are beginning to discover the beauty and strength of their own inner world. More and more, we human beings are realizing the need to develop the power of the mind, as we try to keep up with the ever-increasing pace of life and its complexities.

These nine lessons are based on the teachings of the Brahma Kumaris World Spiritual University, an international organization offering people of all backgrounds an opportunity to learn meditation and deepen their understanding of themselves. The lessons can be practiced alone with great benefit, and there are a number of specific meditations to help the reader bring the theory into practice. However, it would be particularly beneficial to study the lessons in conjunction with attending the free course in meditation at any one of the spiritual university's 4,000 centers worldwide. The atmosphere at these centers and the experience of other meditation practitioners greatly enhance the experiences and understanding gained from the study of this book. By introducing meditation into your own practical life, you not only gain real peace of mind, but also a more positive and healthy attitude toward life.

Sister Jayanti

European Director, Brahma Kumaris

1

Why Meditate?

People want a variety of things from meditation. Some come for peace, others for self-control, some for power and some for silence, but, of all the reasons, the ones which are most often expressed are peace or peace of mind. At first sight there doesn't seem to be much difference between the two, but on closer inspection, we find that they are asking for different things. Peace is simply an experience, whereas peace of mind is a way of life.

At some time or other we have all enjoyed a moment's peace, however fleeting. Simply to experience peace is not actually so difficult. Peace is something easily attainable through the practice of meditation because this is what meditation is specifically designed to give. However, to attain peace of mind implies that you want to experience peace constantly. While you go about your daily life, you need to be in control of yourself to the extent that you can have whatever experience you choose when you choose. To experience constant peace of mind, you need something more than just a meditation technique. After all, in the middle of a dispute with the bus driver over change, you can't just sit yourself down and spend five minutes delving into the deep recesses of the self to regain that temporarily lost inner peace. It is the experience of peace, previously gained through meditation, which you need to be able to use later on in your practical life, especially at times when it is not easy to be peaceful. If you can't use meditation to bring benefit to your daily life, is it really of any use to you?

Therefore, the emphasis in this meditation course will be a double one:

First, to teach a simple, effective method of meditation called Raja Yoga, and to discuss and experiment with ideas on how to deepen the experiences gained.

Second, to look at the reasons behind stress and tension in your life so that, through understanding, you can begin to change the root causes using the power gained through meditation; and also to clarify how you can translate peaceful feelings into peaceful actions, so that peace becomes peace of mind.

What is meditation?

Meditation is the process of getting to know yourself completely, both who you are *inside* and how you react to what is *outside*. Above all, meditation is enjoying yourself in the literal sense of the word. Through meditation, you discover a very different "me" from perhaps the stressed or troubled person, who may seem superficially to be "me." You realize that your true nature, the real you, is actually very positive. You begin to discover an ocean of peace right on your own doorstep.

There is a lovely Indian story about a queen who

had lost her valuable pearl necklace. In great distress, she looked everywhere for it, and just when she was about to give up all hope of ever finding it, she stopped and realized it was right there around her own neck! Peace is very much like this. If you look for it outside in your physical surroundings or in other people, you will always be disappointed; but, if you learn where and how to look for peace within yourself, you will find that it has been here all the time.

The word *meditation* is used to describe a number of different uses of the mind, from contemplation and concentration to devotion and chanting. The word itself is probably derived from the same root as the Latin word *mederi*, meaning "to heal".

Meditation can certainly be looked on as a healing process, both emotionally and mentally, and to a certain extent, physically too. The simplest definition of meditation is: the right use of the mind or positive thinking. It is not to deny thoughts, but to use them correctly. Most forms of meditation employ two main practices:

- concentration exercises, often using an object such as a flower or a candle, and
- the repetition of a mantra.

A mantra is a sacred phrase, word or sound which is repeated constantly, either loudly, silently or in thoughts only. It translates literally as *man* (mind) and *tra* (to free); so, a mantra is that which frees the mind. Raja Yoga meditation does involve concentration, but no physical object is involved. The object of concentration is the *inner* self. Instead of repeating one word or phrase, as in a mantra, a flow of thoughts is encouraged, thus using the mind in a natural way.

This positive flow of thoughts is based on an accurate understanding of the self, and so acts as a key to unlock the treasure-trove of peaceful experiences lying within.

Meditation Practice

Sit in a comfortable position with the back straight. You can either sit cross-legged on a cushion on the floor or, if this is uncomfortable, sit on a chair. Choose a quiet place away from noise or visual distraction. Gentle background music may be played, as this helps to create a relaxed, light atmosphere. Position the book in front of you and read over the following words slowly and silently. Aim to experience and visualize the words in your mind so that you begin to feel what is being described.

Thoughts for Meditation

Let me imagine that nothing exists outside this room. . . .

I feel completely insulated from the outside world and free to explore my inner world. . . .

I turn all my attention inward, concentrating my thought energy on the center of the forehead. . . .

I feel a sense of detachment from my physical body and the physical surroundings. . . .

I become aware of the stillness around me and within me. . . .

A feeling of natural peacefulness begins to come over me. . . .

Waves of peace gently wash over me, removing any restlessness and tension from my mind. . . .

I concentrate on this feeling of deep peace . . .

just peace. . . .

I . . . am . . . peace. . . .

Peace is my true state of being. . . .

My mind becomes very calm and clear. . . .

I feel easy and content . . .

having returned to my natural consciousness of peace. . . .

I sit for a while, enjoying this feeling of calmness and serenity. . . .

Plan to practice repeating these or similar thoughts to yourself for about ten minutes at least twice a day. The best time is in the morning after a bath or shower, before you begin your day's activities. Another good time is in the evening, when your day's activities are over. During the day, while performing any activities, keep reminding yourself:

"Peace is my true nature."

As you keep practicing this meditation, such positive and peaceful thoughts will enter the mind more and more easily, and peace of mind will become increasingly natural.

2

Who Am I?

his simple question seems easy to answer at first. However, as soon as you start to think about it, you realize that giving your name or a description of your physical appearance does not describe the myriad of thoughts, moods, actions and reactions which comprise yourself and your life. Even a description of what you do becomes confusing, because every day you wear so many different hats. You may start the day as a wife or a husband. At work you may be a secretary, a clerk or a teacher. At lunch you may meet a friend and in the evening an acquaintance. Which of these roles that you play is you?

In each role that you play, a different facet of your personality emerges. Sometimes you might feel that you have to play so many different and opposing roles that you no longer know what sort of person you are. When you meet your boss at a party or your parents and friends come to visit at the same time, you become confused as to how to behave. Not only have you fixed yourself a special way of acting toward them, but in your mind you have also limited them to a certain role. You are only able to relate to them as "your boss" or "your parents," not as simply other human beings. Yet you are quite aware that your true identity is not defined by the role you play. How can you think of yourself? Who are you really?

What is needed is something constant, safe and stable. We get up in the morning, look in the mirror and we seem to be much the same as we were yesterday. But we all know that this is an illusion, because gradually, over time, the body is declining; it is not stable or constant. In Raja Yoga, instead of adopting this obvious bodily identification, we start with our thoughts, awareness or consciousness and identify with that, because our thoughts are always there, whatever age we are. Their content may change, but our ability to think does not.

First of all, you are a thinking, experiencing being. Thoughts are not something physical which you can experience with the physical senses. You cannot see, taste or touch a thought. Thoughts are not made up of matter or even brain cells. You are a non-physical or spiritual being. The terms *self* or *soul* are used to describe this.

Your form is the only form that cannot be destroyed. It is something so small that it cannot be divided. It is something without any physical dimension. You, the soul, are a subtle star, a point source of light energy and consciousness. This subtle form is the source of everything that you do—all thoughts, all words, all actions. Whatever you do or say, it is you, the soul, who is performing that action through your body. The soul is like a driver and the body is the car. To be in complete control, the driver has to sit in the place where he has access to the controls and also can collect all the necessary information to make decisions. Each thought, leading to words and actions, begins with an impulse from the brain. In Raja Yoga it is considered that the soul is located in the center of the forehead in the vicinity of the brain. This knowledge provides you with a constant point of reference on which to focus your attention.

Your identity is a soul, and all the other identities—teacher, student, man, woman, father, mother, friend, relation and so on—are simply different roles which you, the soul, play. Good actors can play any role. They will play their roles to the best of their ability, but will never actually think: "I am Hamlet" or "I am Cleopatra." They know that however involved they are with their roles, at the end of the performance they will take off their costumes and resume their true identities. So, whatever role you, the soul, are required to play, you should understand that your true identity is a soul—a living, spiritual, eternal being. The body is simply your temporary physical costume.

The soul has innate, peaceful, positive qualities. In meditation you can create an awareness of yourself as a soul. This naturally leads to an experience of these peaceful, positive qualities. This is what is called *soul-consciousness*. It is not just something to experience while in meditation, but also as you perform action. As you become more aware of who is performing each action, you gain greater control over your thoughts, feelings, words and actions. The natural consciousness of yourself as a peaceful being then fills all your actions, and the desire for peace of mind is fulfilled in a completely practical way.

In meditation you begin to think about your true identity. You let thoughts about the soul and its qualities fill your mind. Initially it doesn't matter how fast the thoughts arise as long as they are moving in the right direction. If your thoughts wander away, gently bring them back again to peaceful thoughts of the self. As you become involved in the experience of such thoughts, they will gradually start to slow down, and soon you will be able to savor them. Just as when you are given something special to eat, you eat it slowly, appreciating each mouthful for its flavor and texture, so you begin to appreciate the experience contained in each positive thought.

The simple phrase *I am a peaceful soul* comes to life as you begin to experience it.

This is a very different approach to meditation from repeating a mantra or focusing on a candle or the rhythm of the breath. In Raja Yoga, sitting meditation is complemented by maintaining a peaceful soul-conscious state while performing everyday actions.

Through maintaining soul-consciousness in this way, you will continue to progress toward your aim of attaining constant peace of mind. A mantra is used purely for sitting meditation. In Raja Yoga, however, you will bring your thoughts in meditation directly into your daily life. This is the first and most important step in making meditation practical. As you go around doing things, you experience being a soul, acting a role through the body. Your consciousness becomes detached from your body. When you see another human being, you look beyond the name, body, race, culture, sex or age and see, with the vision of equality, a soul like yourself who is simply playing a different role. This will help you to develop the qualities needed to remain peaceful all the time, such as tolerance, patience and love.

Through understanding and experiencing your true qualities, you regain confidence and self-respect and are no longer pushed and pulled by the expectations of others. By remaining soul conscious, you will stay in your true state of peace. This is something which does, of course, take time and patient effort to practice. The reward of practice is enjoyable in itself, and the greater benefits will accumulate over time.

Meditation Practice

When you sit to meditate, choose the quietest place you can find, preferably in a room which you do not use very often. If this isn't possible, sit where the familiar objects around you won't distract your attention. Set this place aside, purely for the purpose of meditation. This mental preparation will help your concentration. Start with ten or fifteen minutes. This will gradually lengthen naturally with experience. Soft or subdued lighting will help. A meditation commentary tape can be used to guide the mind in a positive direction. These tapes are available from any Brahma Kumaris Center.

When you finish your meditation, just take a moment to reflect on what you have experienced;

note how your mood has changed. This will emphasize your experiences and help you to appreciate what you are gaining through meditation. One more suggestion of great benefit is: Don't just meditate when you feel like it. The greatest progress is possible at the time when you really don't want to meditate or when you feel you can't. That's the time when you need to meditate the most!

Thoughts for Meditation

I withdraw my attention from my physical limbs and senses. . . . I focus on myself. . . .

I am listening through these ears. . . .

I am looking through these eyes. . . .

I am behind these eyes . . .

in the center of the forehead . . .

an eternal spark of life energy. . . .

This life energy empowers the body. . . .

I am a non-physical being . . .

an eternal soul. . . .

I am the actor. . . .

This body is simply my costume. . . .

*I focus my thoughts on the point in the center of the
    forehead . . . a tiny point of conscient light. . . .*

I feel completely detached from the body . . .

peaceful and light. . . .

I am a star radiating light. . . .

I find deep peace and contentment within. . . .

I now know my true self . . .

an eternal, pure, peaceful soul. . . .

I am in the ocean of peace. . . .

All conflict finishes. . . .

*A deep, deep silence comes over me. . . . Om
    shanti.*

Om, (I am), and *shanti*, (peace): "I am a peaceful
soul."

These thoughts are only a suggestion. Create your
own similar thoughts if you prefer. Any thoughts
based on the awareness of the self as a soul are valid.
Think slowly and aim to experience each thought
before moving on.

3

Soul-Consciousness

hy should the thought, "I am a peaceful soul" be any more beneficial to you than the thought, "I am a body"? In the previous lesson I mentioned that this thought allows you to become detached from the role that you play. It is important to understand what is meant by this word "detached." It does not mean distant or inward-looking to the point of isolation, where there is a breakdown in communication. Nor does it mean that you become an uncaring observer of what is going on. It simply means to have the consciousness of being an actor. You play your part with great enthusiasm and love, but you do not let the expectations, burdens and worries of outside situations or other people affect your own understanding of who you are—a peaceful being. In fact, the word most often used in conjunction with "detached" is "loving". By being aware of yourself as a soul, you can experience your natural qualities so that the feelings you associate with detachment are not of distaste or lack of concern, but of peace, love and happiness.

How can soul-consciousness help you improve your attitude toward yourself and others? We often have the habit of comparing ourselves to others, seeing ourselves in the light of what we consider to be their merits or demerits. This can sometimes lead to a feeling of hopelessness, self-criticism and other equally negative states of mind. Through the experience of soul-consciousness, you will come to realize your own worth and stop comparing yourself with others. You will overcome self-criticism as you experience your true positive qualities and nature. This leads not to a feeling of superiority, but to a feeling of stability and self-confidence. Doubts in the self are replaced by a deeper faith in yourself.

If you understand that you are a peaceful soul, you will understand that others must also be that. Through this awareness, you will be able to relate to them on purely equal terms; that is, with what can be called the vision of brotherhood. Sometimes actions are totally opposed to this. Someone may get angry with you and you feel threatened, replying sharply in return. Thus, a heated argument can develop. This is a reflection of body-consciousness. Instead of primarily seeing the other as a peaceful soul playing a part, you see only the part and think it is the other's true nature.

If, instead, you have the determined thought to see others as souls, you will respond very differently to their anger. You will see their anger as being something temporary and not intrinsic to their true nature. Instead of reacting angrily or being defensive, you will actually become detached or even giving. You can put yourself, quite naturally, into the position of being able to help them. You will recognize that their anger is only to do with their own confusion. This positive attitude acts as protection for you; you then don't feel under attack. In addition, your stable, calm reaction will help to defuse the situation.

There are other ways in which soul-consciousness
can help you to help others. One cannot give what
one doesn't have oneself. When friends come to us
in distress, often the most we can do is give sympa-
thy. Although this is reassuring, it is not necessarily
very helpful. When in trouble, what people need
most is power and clarity. The situation has caused
weakness and confusion in their minds, making it
difficult for them to see things clearly. If your reaction and suggestions to them are not only sympa-
thetic, but also filled with peace, power and
practicality, they can take with them not only comfort, but something which will be of positive value
in helping them to solve their problems. A strong
and uncluttered mind is needed for this.

Soul-consciousness also allows you to be natural
in the company of others. This easiness on your part
helps them to relax, as they don't feel that you have
expectations of them. With soul-consciousness you
aim only to see the good in others, to see not just
apparent virtues, but hidden ones as well. This, in
turn, helps others to realize their own positive

virtues and specialities. A deepening love and respect for other souls naturally will develop as you recognize your spiritual kinship with them. There is the realization that we are all part of one global family, sharing one world, one home.

Meditation Practice

Meditation is being in the awareness of your natural qualities. It is not a difficult thing. Nor is it something that you impose on yourself. You can't force yourself to meditate. In fact, the more hard effort you put in, the less likely you are to experience anything. Too much concentration will create a headache, and instead of refreshment and relaxation, there will be tension.

The first step is simply to relax. Many people would consider being able to relax at will as quite an achievement in itself. In meditation, once you become relaxed, the worries and stress of everyday life dissolve away and the mind is free to explore gentle themes. Your world is a creation of your own mind. This is why you fill your thoughts with soul-consciousness; thinking about peace helps you to experience peace.

The more relaxed you are, the deeper that pleasant, restful feeling becomes, until you have reached a powerful state of meditation, enjoying the quietness which is emerging from within. As you progress, meditation becomes much more than a relaxation technique. The object is not just relaxation; it is to become a peaceful person, to fill yourself completely with peace. The experience of peace, gained through simple relaxation, is a mere drop compared to the ocean of peace in which you can lose yourself through meditation.

You keep your thoughts or themes very simple in meditation; just two or three carefully chosen ones are enough. You repeat them gently, giving yourself plenty of time to explore the feelings behind them, for example, "Peace is just like sinking into a feather mattress . . .", "Lightness is like floating on a cloud . . .", "Love is a warm, golden glow inside your mind. . . ."

As you become more and more engrossed in such thoughts and experiences, you feel yourself gradually letting go of all worldly thoughts and tensions, until you become light and free.

> *I sit quietly, and can feel my physical body relax. . . .*
> *I let tensions fall away, and I focus within, on my own inner being. . . .*
> *I visualize my eternal identity . . . I am a point of light . . . a shining star, radiating light. . . .*
> *As I focus on this awareness of who I am, I feel the connection with the body becoming one of detachment and love. . . .*
> *I . . . the master . . . of this body. . . separate from this body. . . .*
> *For a few moments, I allow my thoughts to go deep within this point of eternity. . . .*
> *I . . . the eternal being . . . without a beginning, without an end . . . touch eternity . . . I . . . am . . . peace.*

Now I have become soul-conscious, aware of my true nature. It is this lightness of consciousness that

I want to bring into my everyday life, so that, whatever problems and obstacles arise in front of me, I deal with them easily and effectively.

Thoughts for Meditation

For the next few days just take up two or three simple themes or phrases, such as, "I am a peaceful soul," "I am a being of light and love, spreading these feelings to others and the world" and "I am a subtle point of consciousness, so different from the physical body." Repeat these thoughts gently to yourself, allowing them to sink in more and more deeply until your thoughts and your feelings match each other. When this happens, the tension between what you think you should be doing and what you actually are doing disappears, and the soul feels content and full. In addition, practice seeing others as souls, seeing beyond the part to the actor who is playing the part.

4

This Thing Called Mind

The Thing Called Mind

itting down and experiencing peace is one thing; actually using it to transform your life is quite another. A great deal goes on between the intention and the action, and sometimes you might catch yourself saying, "I didn't want to do that, but . . ." or "Sorry, I didn't mean to say that." To be in full control of your life you need not only to know, but also to understand the process through which an intention becomes an action.

For instance, a variety of raw materials goes into a car manufacturing plant: sheet metal, nuts and bolts, electrical wiring, paint and so on. These raw materials can be compared to your experiences and intentions. As the raw materials pass through the plant, they are processed and eventually emerge as cars. However, imagine that there is a consistent fault in the production process. You could set about repairing each car as it comes off the production line, but this would be time-consuming and hard work. It would also be very frustrating, as you would consider that the factory had not been built to produce faulty cars.

Similarly, changing your actions superficially will not bring about profound changes in your life. This can work to a limited extent, but you will be continually faced with "faulty" actions from the "production line," and it will seem like very hard labor with not much reward. Instead, you need to check the raw materials of your experience and also become familiar with the "production process" of your desires and actions. It is not enough for the engineer only to know approximately what happens on the factory floor. To repair a fault he needs a detailed working knowledge of everything that is going on.

The better he understands the machinery, the better he is at identifying and repairing the fault. So, the more you understand about how you work, the easier it is for you to eliminate the actions that you don't want. Through meditation you are checking the raw materials, ensuring that only the best quality is used and making sure that nothing is in short supply.

So, what is the process of manufacture? The first and most obvious thing that comes between an intention and an action is a thought. Thoughts occur in the mind. In Raja Yoga, the mind is not seen as a physical thing but as a faculty of the soul, and therefore, non-physical. Through the mind you imagine, think and form ideas. This thought process is the basis of all your emotions, desires and sensations. It is through this faculty that, in an instant, you can re-live a past experience, produce happiness or sadness, or take yourself to the other side of the world.

When there is the thought, "I want a cup of tea," the relevant actions seem to follow automatically. However, is thought the only link between intention and action? What about the expression, *Think before you speak?* Undoubtedly there must be thought before you open your mouth, or nothing would emerge; so, what is meant here? There seem to be

two aspects to thought. The first is the thought itself;
the second is the awareness and understanding of
that thought. It is the intellect which is used to
understand the thoughts. Through this second faculty
of the soul, you assess the value of what emerges in
the mind. In the expression, *Think before you speak,*
you are being asked to use your intellect and consider whether your thoughts are worth uttering.
Some other functions of the intellect are reasoning,
realization, discrimination, judgment and the exercise of willpower.

Generally, you don't worry too much about what
is going on in your mind. But now, for a few
moments, you want to stop external activity and
watch the internal activity—your thoughts.

*As I look within, I can see how my thoughts show
awareness of sounds outside . . . how they register memo-
ries of things of this morning, of yesterday. . . .*

*I see how they are filled with human images, and the
impact of the people I've been with, the things I've heard,
the feelings and moods of those around me . . . my mind
has been influenced by all of these . . .*

For a moment, I take charge of my mind. . . . I create
an image of a point of light . . . a thought of peace. . . .

I hold this thought, and as I continue to keep it in
mind, it becomes more than a thought of peace. . . . It is
a feeling of peace. . . .

A feeling that gives me comfort . . . and strength . . .
and stays with me as I return to my everyday activities.

The intellect is the most crucial faculty; through the intellect you exercise control over your mind and thus over yourself. The purpose of meditation is to fill the intellect with power, thus making yourself clear-headed and perceptive, as well as developing firm resolve. The intellect is recognized by the effect that it has. For instance, someone explains something and you fail to understand it. So he tries explaining it in three or four different ways, but still you don't understand. Finally the fifth time, you *see the light,* that is, you realize what he means. This realization is the working of the intellect.

Another example might be the process through which you sort out a plan of action to take, when faced with a choice of two or three possibilities.

You weigh the advantages and disadvantages until your power of judgment tells you which plan is the most suitable. Like the mind, the intellect is a subtle non-physical entity and belongs to the soul, not the body.

One of the most important realizations for the intellect to work toward comes in answer to the question, "Who am I?"

I begin to be aware of my eternal form, my form of light. . . .

I, the spiritual being, with awareness, with recognition, am now the master. . . .

I am in charge of my physical body . . . and the master in charge of my own mind. . . .

I can feel the unlimited capacity of my mind . . . and as the master of my mind, I focus this unlimited energy onto the path of peace. . . .

I keep my thoughts focused on peace and truth . . . and my mind creates peace. . . .

I am that point of light . . . and I understand where my thoughts should go . . . the destination is peace . . . the path is peace. . . .

With the power of my mind channelled in this way, I radiate peace into the world. . . . I keep my mind in this one direction, of peace and truth.

There is a third faculty of the soul which comprises the impressions left on the soul by actions we have performed. These impressions can be referred to by the Sanskrit word *sanskaras,* for which there is no simple translation. Habits, emotional tendencies, temperament, personality traits are all built up by sanskaras imprinted on the soul through each action it has performed. Sanskaras create the personality in the same way that individual frames on a feature film make up a story. Every action is recorded, whether it is a physical movement, a word or even a thought. As you live your life, you are making an imprint on the celluloid, the soul. All the thoughts that occur in the mind are due to the sanskaras. Personality, the most fundamental feature of each individual, unique soul, is determined by these sanskaras.

The mind, intellect and sanskaras function together

in a cyclic pattern which determines how you behave, what thoughts you have and even what mood you are in. First, the mind produces thoughts, evidence that the intellect judges. On the basis of that judgment, an action is performed or not performed. The action, or non-action, creates a sanskara which, in turn, becomes part of the evidence in the mind.

A good illustration of this is the formation of a habit such as smoking. The first time you are offered a cigarette, many thoughts, both for and against, arise in the mind: "It's bad for my health," "I wonder what it tastes like," "It is very easy to get addicted," "Everyone else does it" and so on. On the basis of these thoughts, the intellect makes a decision. Let's suppose that it makes the decision to try a cigarette. A sanskara is created by that action and the next time you are offered a cigarette that previous action becomes part of the evidence in the mind, as a memory: "I smoked one before." If you decide to smoke one again, the repetition deepens that sanskara, just like planing a groove in a piece of wood, until eventually the evidence in the mind, urging you to smoke, has become so overwhelming that no evidence for not smoking remains. The intellect has now become very weak, even defunct. There is no longer a choice or judgment to make. There is just the strong thought rising in the mind: "Have a cigarette!" and you perform the action automatically. You are no longer in control; your past actions in the form of sanskaras are ruling your present.

However, I can also use this mechanism to create peaceful, positive sanskaras. As you sit in meditation, you will experience yourself as a peaceful soul. This experience forms a sanskara. The next time you are about to get angry, through force of habit, the mind will present contrary evidence: *I am a peaceful soul*. This forces the intellect to make a decision. As the intellect gains strength of will through meditation, it becomes easier to act on peaceful sanskaras, as opposed to negative sanskaras. Thus the intellect begins to control both the mind and actions. You, the soul, become the master of the present. You are no longer the slave of your past. Gradually you will reach a position where you choose to put into action only those thoughts which will lead you to experience permanent happiness and contentment.

Meditation Practice

Take one aspect of yourself that you want to change. A few times a day, create just one or two very powerful positive thoughts which will help change that negative habit or character trait. Do this with all the energy and enthusiasm you can muster. This will create a very powerful sanskara. When that positive thought for change comes into your mind again, it will bring with it the experience of enthusiasm. This will help you to put that intention into action at the appropriate time. For example, if you want to give up the habit of criticizing people, throughout the day keep creating the positive thought: "I see all as peaceful souls. Instead of criticizing their weaknesses, I will only see their virtues and specialities" or "I must first change my own weaknesses before criticizing the weaknesses of others."

5

Keeping the Balance

o continue to progress toward your aim of attaining constant peace of mind, the most important thing is balance. If a car is too heavily weighted on one side, the driver will find it difficult to control and maneuver. Problems will arise with the tires, suspension and so on. The same can happen to you if you pay too much attention to sitting in meditation, being introverted, and not enough attention to relating peacefully to others. You may become withdrawn, living in your own inner world, instead of the "real world" outside. You may find that relationships with others become difficult.

There are four aspects to bear in mind to avoid such an imbalance. If equal weight is given to all four, you can remain balanced while making natural, easy progress.

These four aspects are: *knowing, being, becoming* and *giving*.

Knowing refers to the understanding of knowledge.

You have been given the basic facts: you are a soul; your true nature is peaceful; you have a mind, intellect and sanskaras. Now you have to fit them together. These facts are like the pieces of a puzzle; it is only when they are fitted together in the correct way that the picture emerges. Each piece has a little bit of a pattern on it; on its own, it can only hint at what the completed picture is. By turning the information over in the mind, playing with it, matching it up to your life as it unfolds, you begin to create a coherent view. Once there is understanding, you begin to feel that you are in control of your situation. When there is understanding, your intellect remains clear, and you are able to act in a positive and effective manner. Knowledge allows you to be detached from potentially stressful situations.

What is it that I now know? I know that my hands

*and feet, my arms and legs, are simply my body parts . . .
they are not me. . . . Even the whole of this body is not
me . . . it is my instrument, or vehicle. . . .*

*But who am I, the one in charge of this instrument?
I now understand how I, the pinpoint of energy, the
point of light within, am the one who uses this
instrument. . . .*

*I, the soul, look out through these eyes. . . . I, the soul,
receive the information coming in through these eyes. . . .
I, the soul, decide to communicate, and so I use this
mouth. . . . I am the one who decides what it is that I wish
to communicate. . . .*

*I, the being of light, have the capacity to decide what
information I pick up through these ears. . . .*

*I am the master of this physical instrument . . . I am
in charge. . . .*

I know . . . who . . . I am.

Being refers to yoga, the experience of meditation.

Even if you can sort out all the logical connections
between the bits of information which you have
received, unless you have a grasp of their true meaning, you cannot really say you have understood

them. For instance, you could learn some simple phrases in Hungarian and be able to repeat them in the correct order; but unless your teacher had explained the meanings of the words, the phrases would be of absolutely no use to you.

So, how are you to understand what words like *peace, love, soul* and *detachment* mean? You understand these concepts only by experiencing them. The experience of peace makes peace a reality. It also gives you a basis of trust and faith, for it is when the concept and the experience coincide that the soul can feel secure. Practical experience of the theoretical knowledge which you have been given verifies the knowledge. This leads to trust in the knowledge; through that trust and sense of truth you build a stable foundation.

> *Stepping back . . . inside my own skin . . . coming to the awareness of the being that I am . . . I explore my original state of being. . . .*

> *Within my being, in my original state, there is cleanliness . . . purity. . . .*

I accumulated dust when I travelled, but when I began my journey, I was clean . . . pure. . . .

As the dust is removed, and that pure, clean state shines through, I can feel peace. . . .

Peace is my natural state of being . . . this is who I am. . . .

In this state of purity . . . and peace . . . I rediscover the love that is within . . . a love that is altruistic . . . love for myself . . . love for each member of my human family . . . love for the Supreme. . . .

Purity, peace, love, and joy . . . these are my natural qualities, my true state of being.

Becoming refers to your actions.

In the last paragraph, harmony between knowledge and experience was emphasized. If there is any contradiction, trust and stability disappear. Again, what is vital here is harmony between what happens internally and what happens externally. To sit in meditation and experience yourself as a peaceful soul, and then immediately afterwards to become

angry with someone, renders that peaceful experience meaningless, and the soul feels lost and confused. Meditation must be made practical; its
positive power must be reflected in action. You will
actually become that which you experience in
meditation.

Putting the results of meditation into practice
must, on the whole, be a conscious thing. It won't
happen miraculously, without your paying attention. It is easy to see why this is true, if we again consider how the soul performs actions through the
cycle of mind, intellect and sanskaras. Even though
you are creating peaceful sanskaras in meditation,
the old peaceless sanskaras will continue to create
negative thoughts in your mind, sometimes very pow-
erfully. It is only through conscious choice within
the intellect that you can discriminate and change
your behavior.

What is important to understand here is that you
will never experience progress unless you make an
effort to change your negative actions and habits.
However good your experiences in meditation are, if

4

they are constantly contradicted by your actions, you will continue to create negative thoughts about yourself; your mind will become a battlefield instead of a haven of peace.

Let me take a journey back to my original state of being, in which I was pure, clean, without a blemish, without a stain. . . .

In that state of cleanliness there was comfort . . . there was peace. . . .

Through my journey, I accumulated a heap of rubbish . . . a huge amount of dust. . . .

And now, I clean out that which doesn't belong to me . . . I become that which I was, that which I am, that which is my true nature. . . .

I connect with my own original form . . . and I act in that consciousness . . . I become that, here and now. . . .

Purity, peace and love are within me . . . I let emerge these qualities . . .

I become clear and clean again.

Giving refers to harmonious and altruistic relationships with others.

Although becoming peaceful automatically helps your relationships with others, you still have to pay attention to this area, mainly because it is your relationships with others that spark off peacelessness within you. It is easy to be friendly and giving when those around you are friendly and giving also. Unfortunately, in today's world, we often find ourselves in interpersonal conflicts, ranging from mildly uncomfortable to openly hostile. In these situations, the practice of giving is your protection. It protects you from experiencing negativity, but also benefits the other soul who is unfortunate enough to be feeling aggressive. You cannot give and receive at the same time; so, thinking only peace and good wishes means there is no room for responses of fear or resentment or the awakening of anger within yourself.

These types of situations are the tests which face you every day. It is how you cope in these instances which is the true measure of your progress. When there is victory, you realize that you truly understand some aspect of knowledge. If, however, you do become angry or get careless, the desire to get it right next time sends you back to review the knowledge for deeper understanding. Sometimes you will be in a position to help others directly by sharing your own positive experiences. When this happens, having put things in your own words will make you realize how much you have understood. Every time you return to the knowledge, you will have moved a little bit further forward. So, natural progress is taking place.

Giving should be done without the desire for return or reward. It should be a natural process, simply motivated by the wish to share with others positive experiences which you have internalized. Feeling happy and content is the natural reward of your positive actions. Without desires and expectations, your giving becomes truly altruistic. When you have practiced meditation for some time, giving becomes something beyond words. The knowledge and meditation experiences will become so much a part of you that simply by being your true positive self, you will give the experience of peace and virtuousness to others.

In the awareness of my original state of being, my original treasures of purity, peace and love emerge fully. . . .

And in a very natural way, whatever I am, whatever I have,

I transmit to the world. . . .

In this awareness of my eternal treasures, I send out good feelings . . . pure feelings . . . towards each member of my human family. . . .

I radiate purity . . . I am a being of peace. . . .

What do I have that I can share with the world? . . . It is peace. . . .

My thoughts . . . my vibrations . . . of peace . . . spread out into the universe. . . .

I contribute to the creation of a world of peace by sharing thoughts of peace. . . .

I am a being of love . . . and I feel this warm glow within me . . . a warmth that comforts and supports and empowers others. . . .

It is not the love of possessiveness or attachment . . . the love that binds me to one or two . . . it is the love that is inclusive, that connects me with the whole world. . . .

I give . . . pure love . . . to my world family.

When all these four aspects of *knowing, being, becoming* and *giving* are in harmonious balance, the soul will be at peace with itself and in harmony with others. This state of practical soul-consciousness has been termed "jeevan mukti" or "freedom in life".

Meditation Practice

Slow down! Give yourself time to think before you act. Give your new peaceful sanskaras a chance to be put into practice. Give yourself permission to have the time to practice. Concentrate during the time you have available. Short periods of regular meditation will increase the benefit which you experience. Naturally, over time, the periods you remain in meditation will lengthen and the benefit will continue to increase.

Practice being detached from your own thoughts. Create the thought: "I, the soul, am in the cinema, watching my thoughts come up on the screen of my mind." As you watch them, they will begin to slow down. Sort through them, discriminating between the positive and the negative or wasteful (mundane) ones. Have action replays of the best thoughts, and allow your thoughts to lead you into the experience which lies behind them.

If you find your mind is still too active or at all negative, first concentrate on that basic thought, "I am a peaceful soul." Observe the direction in which your thoughts flow from that positive source. Sometimes the mind will naturally go in a positive direction when you sit for meditation, but at other times it needs to be firmly steered and guided to avoid crashing into the rocks of negative emotions and thoughts!

6

Karma

While you may have associated yourself completely with your physical body, you may not have realized that every action had such a deep impact on you. Now, with the recognition of the self as a soul, you should become aware that every single action leaves an imprint, a record, which you carry with yourself eternally.

Up until now, we human beings have found it very difficult to classify exactly what is right and what is wrong. Throughout history our definition of right and wrong has been changing. Different cultures and religions came up with different definitions and classifications. Even within the same religion, people of different generations have different ideas of right and wrong. Even if you don't consider the external situation at all, but look within yourself, you will find that your understanding fluctuates a great deal. In childhood, your understanding was on one level; in adolescence it changed; in maturity it has changed yet again.

As you are influenced by the atmosphere or the words of human beings, your intellect wavers in its own judgment. So, can you possibly arrive at a point where you know absolutely what is right and what is wrong? Not while you are limited by this physical costume. The religion into which you were born, as well as the limitations of gender, of age and of culture, will all color your ideas, thoughts and judgment. By maintaining the consciousness of your true identity—a peaceful soul—you are able to understand accurately what is right and wrong. This is simply because, in soul-consciousness, the soul can only experience peace, happiness and love. So, it can only perform actions based on these qualities. These actions will be beneficial actions, bringing happiness and positive results. In body-consciousness there is not the pure intention behind action. Our actions are performed with selfish ulterior motives, such as greed, ego and possessiveness, and are therefore non-beneficial actions which give sorrow and bring negative results. It is the consciousness with which we perform action that is important.

The *Law of Karma*, of action and reaction, is applicable to the spiritual sphere and is absolute. It states: For every action there will be an equal and opposite reaction. *Opposite*, of course, means opposite in direction. Whatever interactions you have with others, you receive the equivalent in return. This means that, if you have given happiness, you will receive happiness in return, and if you have given sorrow, you will receive sorrow in return. The law is simple, and when understood in its full depth, it can give insight into the significance of events in your own world and in the world at large. In Christianity this law has been understood by the saying, *As you sow, so shall you reap.* It is also known as the *Law of Cause and Effect.*

Understanding this, when you see certain effects, there is now the realization that effects can only take place if there is a cause. So karma (action) is the cause, and the fruit of karma is the effect. Generally, when you see the fruits of your karma, you might tend to forget that you are responsible for these effects. If the fruit of karma is bitter rather than sweet, you might point the finger of blame at others and say that others are responsible for your suffering. If there is the effect of sorrow, you now should understand that you have been responsible for the cause of sorrow. Understanding the Law of Karma makes you take total responsibility for your own situation, your state of mind and indeed your whole life.

Sometimes only half the Law of Karma is understood, and this is concerning destiny. Someone may think helplessly: "Whatever is happening to me now is because of my past actions; so, there is nothing I can do about it. It is my fate." When there is understanding of the Law of Karma and awareness that you are responsible for your own situation, you will develop tolerance, acceptance and endurance, qualities which may have been missing before. However, more importantly, the other side of the Law of Karma teaches that, if you now perform pure, beneficial actions, you can create your own positive future in the direction of your choice. Not only are you not a slave to destiny, but the understanding of Karma philosophy makes you the creator or master of your own destiny. You may even be able to inspire others to create a positive destiny for themselves through the example of your own beneficial actions.

Any negativity of the past has led you into "karmic debts" with those around you. Where you have in the past given sorrow, you must now repay that debt by giving happiness. You have to settle your past "karmic accounts." However, just because you change your attitude doesn't necessarily mean others will change theirs. If you have courage and continue to give good wishes and perform pure actions in relation to other souls, gradually the karmic debts with others toward whom you have acted negatively will be repaid. Then you can be free from the bondages of karma.

The power to sustain this effort of settling past karma can come through meditation or yoga. As you come to understand your own true nature more fully, you can understand that this is the true nature of everyone. You can see through the mask of negativity and relate to the soul directly. This will help you not to create further negative karma; you will not react badly to the negativity of others.

I . . . the soul . . . have been performing karma through this physical costume of mine. . . . I carry the imprints of this karma, good and bad. . . . I have been seeing the results of my karma externally, in the world around me. . . .

And now, I come to the awareness of my eternal state . . . a state in which I have no karmic bondage. . . .

This is the state I want to attain once more . . . the state of freedom . . . the state of having settled all my karmic debts, and of having created for myself a stock of good karma. . . .

In this awareness of I, the eternal being, I look back at the past and see the entangled threads of karma. . . .

Where did a connection begin? Where did it finish? The threads are so intertwined . . . it's difficult to differentiate. . . .

The web of karma has been one in which there has been a lot of pain . . . a few flashes of light, of hope, of joy . . . but the negativity of my karma created situations in which there was much suffering. . . .

Now, at this moment, in the presence of the divine, I let go of my karma of the past. . . .

With God's love, I surrender my past karma to God . . . and I take light and might from the Supreme . . . so that my karma today will create a future filled with light. . . .

God's light shows me the path of righteous karma. . . . God's might . . . God's power . . . gives me the courage to reject negative karma and even mundane karma. . . .

I simply do that which is elevated and noble . . . so that my present is filled with light and might . . . and a future of happiness and love is assured.

With soul-consciousness you will naturally give love and respect to others, and you will, in time, receive love and respect in return. Every action performed in soul-consciousness is an action through which you receive benefit, and thus it will benefit others. Karma begins in the mind as thoughts, the seeds of action. As is the thought, so is the result. Thoughts, like actions, spread vibrations and influence the surrounding atmosphere. Karmically there will be a return of those vibrations. Pure, peaceful, happy thoughts are the most valuable treasure of life. If you keep such beneficial thoughts in your consciousness wherever you go, you will create a pure atmosphere of peace and happiness, from which others will greatly benefit.

Understanding the consequences of actions means you take care to do everything properly. Having little control over your actions is a sure sign that you have little control over your mind. This links up with the last lesson; if you slow down, you give yourself more time to do things properly. If something is done well, the likelihood is that it won't cause problems in the future. Jobs done in a rush often contain mistakes which have to be put right later, thereby causing more work. A good job done well leaves you with a peaceful mind. A careless piece of work pulls your attention back to itself again and again. If you concentrate completely on what you are doing in the present, this allows you to be in full control of both mind and body. You keep performing actions in soul-consciousness so that, no matter how much you have to do physically, you can remain light and peaceful.

Meditation Practice

Divide into three segments your time for sitting in meditation.

Take three meditation themes or positive qualities which follow on from each other, such as: stillness, silence and power; and lightness, peace and contentment.

Take each theme separately, creating thoughts that will lead you into the experience of each quality. Make sure that you have achieved an experience of the first quality before moving onto the second, and the second before moving onto the third. In this way you can gently lead yourself into deeper experiences in meditation, as well as enjoying a variety of positive feelings and qualities.

7

The Supreme

Throughout history, we human beings have sought many things. Above all we have desired two things: happiness and a perfect relationship. If we have achieved either one or both of these things, it has been a constant struggle to keep them. They have usually proved to be temporary. If we want to achieve them on a permanent basis, we must look beyond the limited gains of possessions, money and fragile human relationships.

Raja Yoga has two meanings: *Sovereign Yoga*, the yoga through which you can become the sovereign, the master of yourself; and the *"Supreme Union,"* or *"Union with the Supreme."* This second aspect of Raja Yoga involves developing a relationship with the Supreme, the source of perfection, God. Within this yoga or union you can fulfill your wish for inner happiness and your desire for a perfect relationship.

It does not even require that you first believe in God. It is useful to simply have an openness to the idea that there may be a greater source of spiritual energy than yourself. Through your own experimentation in meditation you can develop an understanding of this concept. If someone asked you, "Do you believe in the existence of Mr. X?," you would be inclined to want to meet him first, before committing yourself. Under the circumstances, you would keep an open mind. Similarly, with the concept of a supreme spiritual energy, until there is direct experience, it would be unwise to commit oneself. Yet, if you want to have contact with the Supreme Being, there are certain things that you must know. First, you should know the form of the Supreme so that you will be able to have accurate recognition. Second, you need to know what "language" to use so that there can be communication. Third, you need to know where your meeting can take place.

In Raja Yoga, just as we have a very precise notion of the form of the soul, so we also have a very precise notion of the form of the Supreme. In fact, the Supreme is recognized as the Supreme Soul. So, he has a form identical to that of the human soul, that is, a point source of consciousness, a spark of light energy.

When we use the word *he*, this is not to imply that we think of the Supreme as male. The soul itself has no gender; it is only the body that has gender. Whereas the human soul takes a body, the Supreme Soul never has a body of his own, and so, is neither male nor female.

God never takes human birth. So, he never forgets his original qualities as we do. He remains eternally peaceful, blissful and powerful. Our experience of our own original qualities is limited.

God is eternally the unlimited ocean of virtues. He is completely full, and so never needs anything. This means he is totally benevolent, ever-giving. In fact, within Raja Yoga we have a particular name for the Supreme, and that is Shiva Baba. Shiva means benevolent. He is the only being who is truly altruistic, whereas we humans normally look for something in return, even if it is only the pleasure of giving. God gives without any desire or expectation of return. Baba is a sweet and familiar name for father; thus, Shiva Baba is the benevolent Father of all souls.

The reason Father is used is because of the concept of a father giving an inheritance to his children. In this case, the inheritance received is of peace, love, knowledge and happiness. The Supreme is also the Mother, the Friend and the Beloved. In fact, whatever relationship or positive role you wish to see in him, you can, because he is the unlimited source of all qualities, both male and female. So, whatever the situation, you always have a source of help and strength to draw on; a source that is only a thought away.

How can you communicate with this being? Meditation is about experiencing yourself, experiencing your own qualities. You create peaceful thoughts in order to experience peace. Paradoxically, the more you absorb yourself in that peace, the fewer thoughts you need. The communication with the Supreme is on this level. You come to know him through the experiences that you have of his qualities. You begin to feel those qualities surround you. My communication with God is primarily through silent experience. In deep silence you can lose yourself in the Ocean of Peace. With this experience you feel refreshed. You begin to understand your own qualities and specialities more deeply, and this brings confidence. You take power, which enables you to maintain a peaceful stage while going about your daily life.

In the awareness of my eternal identity . . . I, the soul, become aware of an eternal connection . . . not only with all the human souls around me, but also with a being who is the Supreme. . . .

A soul . . . a being of light . . . with a form that is infinitesimal . . . and yet from that point of light, a radiance of infinite peace, love, joy. . . .

In the awareness of my own original state of peace . . . I can tune in . . . and connect with the Ocean of Peace. . . .

Waves of peace from the Ocean of Peace reach me and surround me . . . peace filled with sweetness . . . peace filled with strength. . . .

I, the child of the Supreme, realize that this is my eternal Parent . . . This is the one who gives constant love, support, protection. . . .

This is my Parent who constantly cares for me, sustains me and guides me . . . the Ocean of Unlimited Love. . . .

This is the Being who is the Bestower, the Absolute, able to give constantly, and so needing no return. . . .

One who is benevolent, the Supreme Benefactor . . .

Through my thoughts, I stay connected with the Supreme . . . I fill myself from the Ocean . . . I reclaim my original nature of peace, love, and joy. . . .

You also need to know where to find him. When you sit in meditation and go deep within yourself, a feeling of stillness comes over you. In that silence, your experience is that you are in an unchanging world, a timeless world. Yet this physical world is ever-changing. If your consciousness is tied to the physical, you can never get away from the passage of time. It is as though you have taken your consciousness beyond this world to another world. We call this place the soul world, the original home of the soul. It is a timeless world of silence and stillness, full of peace and power, a world of infinite golden-red light. This is also the home of the Supreme Soul. Taking yourself there, you begin to experience his unlimited qualities of peace, love, purity, bliss and power surrounding you. Through this most perfect of all relationships, you take power and guidance so that you can clear your karmic debts of the past and create a peaceful, happy and stable future.

As I connect with One, the magnetism and power of the Supreme lift my consciousness beyond the physical dimension . . . into a world of light. . . .

I find myself in a place of infinity . . . a region where there are no borders . . . a place of stillness . . . of silence . . . of perfect purity. . . .

This is my home . . . a place where I feel so comfortable, so at peace . . . I am with my Supreme Parent . . . I belong to this Mother and Father . . . to this home. . . .

I experience my original state of stillness, of purity, in my home. . . .

This is a place of rest. . . .

Down below, the world stage is a place of action, and

I will journey back there in a few moments. . . .

But for now, I can be up here in my home . . . with my Parent . . . learning to be the observer . . . learning to be free. . . .

Meditation Practice

Sitting in a quiet and relaxed atmosphere, slowly read over the following thoughts about the relationships one can have with the Supreme.

Thoughts for Meditation

When I meet the Supreme in the land beyond sound and movement, the only things that exist are the feelings in my heart.

It is my open heart that God reads.

He knows what it is I truly desire.

He fulfills that need.

What is required of me is honesty, cleanliness and clarity in my own mind to enjoy fully this meeting with my Supreme Father—Baba. Baba fulfills my deepest needs and wishes in many ways through many relationships.

As the Father, God gives me love and understanding.

As his child, I have the spiritual birthright to his inheritance, the unlimited treasure-store of all his perfect virtues and powers.

I also experience the sweetness and comfort of God as the Mother, in whose lap the soul can rest in tenderness and care.

I can share all my thoughts and hopes with Baba, my Friend, and even my doubts and problems, for there is nothing to hide from a true friend.

I can enjoy a heart-to-heart conversation at any time I wish, in any place.

As the Teacher, God fills me with truth.

He has an answer for every question, advice for every need, revealing to the self all the secrets of time and eternity, unravelling the mysteries of creation, so that the meaning of life becomes so clear . . . for in God I have found the perfect teacher, the source of truth . . . and he is also my liberator and guide, freeing the self from all sorrows and suffering . . . guiding me along the path to freedom and happiness. . . .

As my one Beloved, God is the comforter of my heart.

With God as my Beloved, the search for true love

ends and the experience of contentment and com-
pleteness begins.

Having the experience of all these relationships with
God provides me with everything I need . . .

. . . fulfilling all my pure desires and dreams.

The seed of all these relationships is love.

Behind every thought and action of his is pure love
and the wish only to bring benefit to the soul . . .
to uplift . . . to purify me.

God's love is unlimited and endless.

8

Time Waits for
No One—or Does It?

ir Isaac Newton set up a picture of a clock-work world, ticking away inside a cosmic clock. Time was an absolute thing. A second was a second, no longer, no shorter. Wherever we are, in our living room or on a pulsar millions of light years away, whatever we are doing, it ticks away, independent of any outside influences. This is a common sense view of time, and if we thought like this, we would be thinking along the same lines as western scientists did for nearly three hundred years after Newton.

Then, at the beginning of this century, an enigmatic figure called Einstein presented a theory, the implications of which rocked the foundations of three centuries of work. This was the theory of relativity. Part of what Einstein said was that the only way one can measure time is by clocks, be they water clocks which drip every second or mechanical clocks which tick. Basically all clocks move, and therefore, time is dependent on movement; time is not totally independent. He wasn't the first person to think like this; he was, however, the first person to formulate a usable mathematical theory about it (containing that famous equation, $E = mc_2$). To understand this clearly, let's return to Newton's theories. What Newton said was that there is a cosmic clock out there ticking away, against which one can measure things. This clock of Newton's isn't a "real" clock, but it's like a solid idea. Time is passing by, independent of whatever is happening. Now let's do a little experiment. Imagine that we all go to sleep one night, and when we wake in the morning, everything is moving at half speed. According to Newton, "real" time is still ticking away up there, and, in fact, we are taking twice as long to do everything. In the final reckoning, a "nine-to-five" job has not taken eight hours, but sixteen hours.

Einstein says that we have no way of knowing, when we wake up on the morning after this strange event, that everything is working at half its previous speed. There is no real time there, by which to measure everything that happens. Time is a measure of our activities. If all the timepieces in the world have slowed down to half speed, then time itself has slowed down to half speed. In other words, Newton's time is rigid and Einstein's time is elastic.

When we woke up that morning, everything would have seemed normal. We wouldn't have felt that everything had slowed down, because the only way to judge that would have been by comparing it with something else which had not slowed down. In other words, things would still be moving at the same speed relative to each other. How can these two ideas help you practically? First, according to how you regard time, you are either its master or its servant. With a Newtonian outlook you become its servant, as "time waits for no one," and so you feel that you have to rush around, cramming as many activities as you can into every relentless second. Now, let us consider how it is more helpful to have Einstein's view of time.

In this case, time is dependent on rate of change. What is the changing thing within yourself whose speed is going to govern how fast time appears to be moving? It is your own thoughts. If you slow your thoughts down, time will appear to expand. If you speed them up, time contracts. It's not that you slow your thoughts down in the same way you would slow down a record; you simply leave space between each thought or even between each word. You then become aware, not only of the thoughts, but also of the free spaces. Awareness of these peaceful spaces between thoughts brings you right into the present and gives you the feeling that there is room to maneuver, time to spare.

When you first approach something new—for instance, the first time you use a particular recipe— you read each instruction carefully. Then, thinking only about that, you perform the relevant action, returning to the cookbook again only after you have completed it. This mode of operation makes sure that everything is done correctly and the best possible result is attained. Having given yourself time and space to do the job well, on completion of the task, you feel satisfied.

Compare this with the situation where the instructions, in the form of thoughts, follow each other in rapid succession, not waiting for each instruction to be put into action before the next one arises. The result is that, as you are doing one thing, your mind is badgering you to get on and do the next thing. You feel under pressure. You feel that you do not have enough time to do all the actions correctly. Consequently, on completion, you often find that the job has not been done well. Instead of a feeling of satisfaction, there is stress and tension. So, it is not just the speed of thoughts that is important, but the speed of thoughts relative to actions. If the speed of your thoughts (your instructions to yourself) matches the speed with which you can do things, you will remain free from stress and tension and you will feel that there is time to do things properly. The effect of this is that you feel as though you are *creating* time for yourself.

Another advantage which immediately becomes

apparent when this is practiced is the ease with which actions and reactions can be controlled. Great sportsmen have control over their minds when practicing their sport. This is clearly visible with someone like Michael Jordan; so precise and clear are the instructions he gives to his body that each step he takes or shot he makes seems effortless and totally economical. There is no wasted physical effort.

The spaces we leave when we slow our thoughts down allow us to change direction easily and immediately. When thoughts race, it's as though they gather momentum like a car going at full speed. If we are required to make an unexpected left turn, we then have to slam on the brakes, upsetting ourselves and the people in the cars behind us. We will probably overshoot the turning and have to waste time and effort, reversing and finally making the correct maneuver. When this happens in our minds, the emergency stop leaves us shaken and confused, and can be disturbing to those around us. However, the spaces between thoughts are like times when we are temporarily stationary. From a stationary position we can move in any direction we choose, smoothly and easily, without causing discomfort to anyone.

This practice of slowing thoughts down and giving ourselves more time is helpful in many ways. Above all, it allows us to be soul-conscious much more easily. Those spaces give us time to enjoy sweet feelings of peace and contentment, which are natural qualities of the soul.

Undoubtedly, Newtonian time is the sort of time which governs the physical world around us. Without this solid framework to refer to, things would be most disturbing. However, through Einstein's "window," you can escape this physical world and fly to that timeless expanse, the soul world. This highest dimension is timeless, as there is no movement, just constant stillness. In your spiritual home you can learn how to slow your thoughts down to such an extent that they stop altogether, and now, in total silence, stillness and contentment, you discover the beauty of eternity.

Meditation Practice

Practice the habit of saying "Past is past." Keep facing forward. If something negative happens, don't feel guilty about it. Simply have the determined thought to conquer it. Re-channel the energy that usually goes into guilt or regret into positive thought and willpower, so that the soul says: "Yes, I am making efforts to change and improve myself."

Thoughts for Meditation

I experience myself as a bodiless being . . . a source of light, peace and power in a world of light. . . .

I feel that everything is totally still . . . timeless . . . Nothing is changing.

There is the experience of deep contentment. . . .

There is nothing more that the soul desires. . . .

I am with God in my eternal home of silence. . . .

I absorb the Ocean of Peace. . . .

I remain with the unlimited source of all virtues and fill myself totally.

I am overflowing with light and peace . . . spreading the qualities of the Supreme into this world.

The Eight Powers

ight powers are specifically mentioned as being developed through Raja Yoga. At first they might seem like eight qualities, but the word *power* has been used, in this context, for a particular reason. What is the difference between a quality and a power? A quality is something which others can sometimes see in us, but it is also sometimes hidden. It is something which others appreciate, but do not necessarily feel that they can possess. A power is something that cannot remain hidden; it is a constant source of inspiration to others so that they too can change themselves and become powerful.

The eight powers are:

INTROVERSION, or the power to turn within

The power to LET GO of thoughts of the past that are no longer useful

The power to TOLERATE

The power to ACCOMMODATE, or adjust to situations and people

The power to DISCERN, or discriminate between true and false

The power to JUDGE priorities and make decisions

The power to FACE obstacles or losses

The power to COOPERATE with others

It is important not just to know what these powers are, but even more importantly to understand when and how to use them. For instance, if you are constantly tolerating someone's bad behavior and the situation is getting steadily worse, perhaps you should really be using the power to face them, that is, to have the courage to say, in a peaceful but firm way, that such behavior is not acceptable. The eight powers are such that in any situation, there will be at least one power that is appropriate for your use. The correct choice of that power will depend on your remaining calm and having a clear picture of the situation in question.

1. **The power to turn within** is the foundation of

all the powers. It brings the strength to remain peaceful and positive while in the midst of life's challenges. Naturally, your thoughts must be concentrated and engaged when you perform an activity, but during any task you can also turn your thoughts within and practice returning to your state of inner peace. In this way, your thoughts do not continue to be involved needlessly, and you waste no mental effort. This is true controlling power, which brings great strength to the soul.

The wind, the rain, the sun, the storms . . . all of this is the nature of the outside world . . . but just as a tortoise turns inside its shell, I turn inwards to the essence of my own being.

I connect with the point of peace that I am. I find that inner balance, that equilibrium, that strength within.

Turning inwards, I connect with truth, with reality. I understand who I am and what I must do.

With my awareness of truth and reality renewed, I step out into the world, now able to perform action with the consciousness of truth.

2. **The power to let go of** wasteful (mundane) thoughts in soul-consciousness means that you can travel light, packing only that which is necessary. Not carrying around negative and wasteful thoughts keeps me free from both mental and physical tiredness.

This economy brings power and a completely positive outlook.

I step out of the cycle of the past, present and future and look at the cycle of time as an observer. . . .

At this one moment, I can see the past . . . I can see the present . . .

I also see the future.

I pack up the things of the past, having learned the lessons that are useful . . . I put away the things that are not necessary, that are no longer required.

I stay with the essence, with truth, with reality, so that my present thoughts are elevated . . . and my actions will be likewise. . . .

When I look into the future there is nothing but

light . . . only light . . . and goodness . . . I learn to love this power of packing up.

3. **The power to tolerate** difficulties involves the ability to go beyond the influence of negative situations, to be able to not react, even in thoughts. If someone offers you insults, criticism or anger, or if there is physical suffering, with the power to tolerate you can remain peaceful and happy. On the basis of soul-consciousness, you will be able to give love, like the fruit tree which, when pelted with sticks and stones, gives its fruit in return.

Connecting with my own inner treasures . . . connecting with the divine source, the Supreme . . . I am filled with the fruits of all attainments. . . .

I have all that I need . . . I am overflowing . . . I have enough to be able to share generously with others.

In situations of attack, I don't respond in kind . . . I respond by sharing the fruits of my attainment.

I give peace where there has been aggression . . . love,

*where there has been animosity . . . compassion, where
there has been insult.*

*A tree laden with fruits will share only fruit, nothing
else . . . I receive the fruits of all attainments from God,
and I share these with the world.*

4. **The power to accommodate** is the power to be
   above any clash of personality or nature, to be
   able to mold and adjust yourself, as the situation requires. You should not be one to create
   conflict in any situation. Just as an ocean can
   accommodate all the rivers flowing into it, so
   you should not reject anyone or anything.
   Instead, you are able to change relationships
   and circumstances through the power of good
   wishes.

*Connecting with the Supreme, I am drawn from the
limited into the unlimited . . .*

*My heart stretches and grows . . . I receive love and
wisdom from the Supreme . . .*

And I am able to be generous.

As an ocean is big enough to accept everything that

flows into it, I too, connected with the Supreme, am able to absorb, to accept, to accommodate . . .

I can adjust to different situations, and personalities, and all the challenges the world brings me . . .

Keeping myself connected with the Unlimited, my capacity to love becomes unlimited.

5. **The power to discern** is the ability to give correct value to the thoughts, words and actions of yourself and others. Just as the jeweler can discriminate false from real diamonds, so you should be able to keep positive, worthwhile thoughts and discard negative, harmful ones. It is the negative thoughts that often cloud true discrimination, and you will eliminate these through meditation.

I become detached from my physical body, stable in the awareness of I, the soul . . . and God's light touches the intellect, and makes it divine. . . .

The dust accumulated on the intellect falls away . . . and the divine intellect sparkles, pure and clean, absolutely free. . . .

Connected with the Supreme, I understand all the different ingredients of a situation . . . all the different facets of the diamond, as well as the flaws . . . the variety of energies in relationships. . . .

This understanding brings light . . . and I can see clearly what is false, and what is beautiful and true.

6. **The power to judge** allows you to make clear, quick, accurate and unbiased decisions. For this, you need to be above the influence of situations and the emotions and opinions of others. You also need a clear understanding of what is right and wrong. Raja Yoga meditation provides this strength and clarity of the intellect through greater self-understanding and a detached perspective.

My connection with the Supreme creates clarity . . . I understand all the components of a situation . . . I have no bias to this person or that person . . . my heart is full, so my judgment is not distorted by desires . . . I can decide between priorities . . . I know what needs to be done . . . the correct path for me to take is clearly lit in front of me.

7. **The power to face** obstacles in life (courage) is developed by meditation, through which you experience your original nature of peace and become detached from the consciousness of the physical costume. You are then able to observe and see beyond problems and difficulties, to discover a positive side to something that seems totally negative; this gives you the strength to face these obstacles.

Connecting with the Almighty Authority, as the child with the Parent . . . I receive as my inheritance all the powers of the Supreme.

I have been transformed and uplifted, so that I, the soul, am the master almighty authority. . . .

I have strength and courage . . . I do not fear the situations that come.

God's power gives me the capacity to face whatever comes my way . . . I am able to remain loyal and true to the path of truth and peace.

Facing all adversity, I remain loyal to my Supreme Companion . . . with the power of his company, I overcome all obstacles. . . .

8. **The power to cooperate** with others requires the vision of soul-consciousness, with which you can see all as your brothers and sisters. This attitude of brotherly vision creates unity and strength within a group. This power of cooperation will make any task seem easy.

God's gifts of all the different powers have been preparing me for this . . . God's strength and light make it easy for me to give and receive cooperation. . . .

Having shed my ego and weakness, I see the speciality of each one in my family . . . I'm able to work with them, cooperate with them.

Coming together with the awareness of the one Supreme, we all give our share of cooperation . . . and the task is accomplished . . . a mountain is lifted.

"I," "my," and "mine" have all melted away . . . only the Father, and the Father's task, remain . . . and with this one thought, we come together . . . to serve.

These eight powers become more and more effective in your life as you become expert in applying them to situations, as required.

In Conclusion

This small book provides a brief introduction to the concepts underlying the study and practice of Raja Yoga meditation. After reading this book, it is important to clarify how you can use this information in a personally meaningful and satisfying way. The aim of Raja Yoga is to provide a means by which you can become the master of your own mind and your own destiny, and thus acquire constant peace of mind. So, it is essential for you to proceed at your own pace in a way which feels comfortable. Above all else, you need to develop faith in yourself.

Having faith in yourself means

having the courage to explore what you are capable of experiencing. Blind faith is not a reliable foundation. If one places trust in things that are not understood, sooner or later that trust is going to be shattered. First, there must be understanding; for this, knowledge is needed. In Raja Yoga very specific knowledge is given. Think about this knowledge, understand it and develop a clear picture in your mind. Think about the implications of being a pure, peaceful soul. What effect will it have on your practical life? How will it affect your relationships with others? Does the Law of Karma provide adequate explanations of current situations in your life and in the world? If God exists, will it be possible to have a relationship with him? Only if you consider the implications of the knowledge will you have some sort of measure against which to place the practical experience of meditation and daily interactions. When you sit in meditation, you can see if your experience matches up to the information you have been given. If you practice soul-consciousness during the day, you can see if this brings the results predicted by the knowledge. There will then be a basis for faith; it will rest on the firm foundation of your own experience, not only in meditation, but in practical life also.

Faith needs an aim. To measure your progress, you need to know where you have come from and where you want to go. Knowing where you have come from is not difficult; knowing where you want to go is more subtle. Knowledge tells you, "I am a peaceful soul" or "Om shanti", but how do you translate this into experience? Deep inside you desire peace, but it is like a half-forgotten memory. That desire for peace is being prompted by a sanskara, a sanskara telling you that you must have had an experience of very deep peace before. You are not aiming for something you have never known before. Your aim is simply to rediscover that forgotten feeling of being so peaceful that you are ever-content. When you experience peace in meditation, it feels so natural and easy. It is an effortless thing. Your aim is to be in that experience constantly. Whatever you are doing, whoever you are speaking to, whatever is happening around you, you remain "Om shanti," lost in the ocean of peace, spreading vibrations of peace to others. Faith needs both understanding and experience to sustain it. So, simply make sure that you combine ongoing study of this knowledge with the practical experience of meditation. In this way your life becomes an inspiring source of positivity and happiness for yourself and for those with whom you interact.

Om shanti

The Brahma Kumaris Centers

To find a center near you, see the Brahma Kumaris
Web site at:

www.bkwsu.com

IN THE UNITED KINGDOM AND IRELAND

LONDON

Global Co-operation House, 65 Pound Lane
London NW10 2HH
Tel: 44 181 727 3300
E-mail: *London@bkwsu.com*

NUNEHAM COURTENAY

Global Retreat Center, Nuneham Park
Nuneham Courtney, Oxford OX44 9PG
Tel: 01865 343 551

EDINBURGH

20 Polwarth Crescent
Edinburgh EH11 1HW, Scotland
Tel: 0131 229 7220

DUBLIN, IRELAND
61 Morehampton Road, Dublin 4, Ireland
Tel: 353 660 3967

INTERNATIONAL HEADQUARTERS
Brahma Kumaris World Spiritual University
PO Box No. 2, Mount Abu, Rajasthan 307501, India
Tel: 91 2974 38261 68
E-mail: *bkabu@vsnl.com*

EUROPEAN HEADQUARTERS
Global Co-operation House, 65 Pound Lane
London NW10 2HH
Tel: 44 181 727 3300
E-mail: *London@bkwsu.com*

AFRICAN HEADQUARTERS
Global Museum for a Better World
PO Box 12349, Maua Close, off Parklands Road
Westlands, Nairobi, Kenya
Tel: 254 2 743 572
E-mail: *bkwsugm@holidaybazaar.com*

AUSTRALASIAN HEADQUARTERS

78 Alt Street, Ashfield, Sydney NSW 2131, Australia

Tel: 61 2 9716 7066

E-mail: *indra@one.net.au*

NORTH AMERICAN HEADQUARTERS

Global Harmony House, 46 S. Middle Neck Road

Great Neck, NY 11021

Tel: 516 773 0971

E-mail: *newyork@bkwsu.com*

SOUTH AMERICAN HEADQUARTERS

R. Estavam de Almeida 53/59

Sao Paulo SP 15114-010, Brazil

Tel: 11 872 7838

About the Author

Sister Jayanti is a spiritual teacher and leader, a pioneer and an emissary for peace. She has a vision and experience that is truly global and deeply spiritual. Perhaps this is because among other factors, she is a child of two cultures. Born in India of Sindhi parents, who migrated to England when she was eight years old, she is a blend of Eastern wisdom and Western education and culture. At the age of nineteen she began her life's path of spiritual study and service with the Brahma Kumaris World Spiritual University. At the age of twenty-one, she dedicated her life to making a difference in the world. She has trained for more than thirty years with some of the world's most remarkable yogis. As a result, she herself is a extraordinary meditator and teacher and has developed a clarity and purity of mind that is exceptional. Sister Jayanti is also a much sought-after speaker around the world. Her natural wisdom and gentle, though powerful, personality have touched and inspired millions of people throughout the world. She is the European director of the Brahma Kumaris World Spiritual University and assists in coordinating the University's activities in more than seventy countries. She is also their representative to the United Nations, Geneva.